WARSAW and WARSZAWA i ワルシャワ

GHETTO ゲット

PL GB D NL I F E J P FIN

Editor: B&M Potyralski
Text by B&M Potyralski
Colour photos by M&B Potyralski
Black&White photos: Archives of Mechanical Documentation
Warszawa na starej fotografii. Warszawa 1960
Warszawa miedzywojenna. Warszawa 1964
Warszawskie getto. Warszawa 1993
Introduction translated by Jan K. Milencki
Revised by Janet Fuchila
Translation of text under photos: "Techkon" sp. z o.o. Congress Service
Copyright (c) by B.M. Potyralscy   Warszawa 2000
ISBN 83-901501-2-3

WARSAW and
WARSZAWA i
ワルシャワ

GHETTO
ゲット

(PL) (GB) (D) (NL) (I) (F) (E) (J) (P) (FIN)

(PL) WARSZAWA

Na podstawie tych kilku fotografii chcemy przedstawić Warszawę po zakończeniu II wojny światowej

1, 2, 3, 4 - wszystkie zdjęcia lotnicze przedstawiają zniszczone centrum Warszawy.

5. Hotel Warszawa - znajdował się na Placu Napoleona, dzisiejszy Plac Powstanców Warszawy. Przed wojną najwyższy budynek w Warszawie, w którym mieściło się Towarzystwo Ubezpieczeń „Prudential".

6. Kościół Św. Aleksandra - znajduje się na Placu Trzech Krzyży, obok którego w 1996 roku powstał hotel Sheraton.

7. Pałac Kultury i Nauki - tuż obok zniszczonego dworca kolejowego Śródmieście (fotografia po prawej stronie u góry) powstał w 1955 roku jako dar ZSRR dla Warszawy.

8. Kościół Św. Krzyża i pomnik Mikołaja Kopernika - kościół znany w Warszawie, również ciekawy dla turystów, ponieważ znajduje się w nim urna z sercem Fryderyka Chopina.

9. Kościół Św. Anny - stoi przy ulicy Krakowskie Przedmieście. W głębi widoczne jest Stare Miasto z kolumną króla Zygmunta III Wazy.

10. Zamek Królewski - którego odbudowę rozpoczęto w latach 70-tych, a która trwa do chwili obecnej. W tle dzwonnica i Kościół Św. Anny.

11. Stare Miasto - ulica Świętojańska z widocznym Rynkiem Starego Miasta - (strona Barssa).

12. Rynek Starego Miasta - strona Barssa.

13. Rynek Starego Miasta - strona Dekerta.

14. Kościół Garnizonowy - znajduje się dokładnie naprzeciw pomnika Powstania Warszawskiego przy ulicy Długiej.

15. Kościoł Św. Floriana - kościół ten jest po drugiej stronie rzeki Wisły obok warszawskiego ZOO przy Alei Solidarności.

16. Teren Getta - widoczny Kościół Św. Augustyna, który był w centrum Getta w latach 1942-1943.

17. Teren Getta - zniszczone główne ulice: Gęsia, Zamenhofa, Nalewki.

18. U zbiegu ulic Zamenhofa i Anielewicza w 1948 roku został odsłonięty pomnik Bohaterów Getta, według projektu Marka Suzina. Płaskorzeźby wykonał Nathan Rappoport.

19. Teren Getta - ogólny widok.

20. Pierwszy pomnik dotyczący tragedii warszawskich Żydow, powstał w 1946 roku w 3 rocznicę wybuchu Powstania Żydowskiego.

21. Dzięki komitetowi polsko-amerykańskiemu została odsłonięta w 1995 roku bryła granitowa poświęcona podziemnej organizacji „Żegota", która podczas okupacji hitlerowskiej w Polsce pomagała Żydom. Pomoc finansowana była przez polski rząd, który przebywał w Londynie.

Pomniki na fotografiach 20, 21 usytuowane są w niewielkiej odległości od pomnika Bohaterów Getta. Z tego miejsca prowadzi „Trakt Pamięci, Męczeństwa i Walki Żydów". Składa się z 19 tablic i bloków kamiennych przedstawiających ważne wydarzenia i Żydów podczas trwania warszawskiego Getta.

22. Bunkier Mordechaja Anielewicza - przy skrzyżowaniu ulic Dubois i Miłej znajduje się kopiec z kamieniem upamiętniającym miejsce, gdzie podczas powstania mieścił się bunkier sztabu Powstania Żydowskiego, tzw. Miła 18. W tym miejscu 8 maja 1943 roku popełnił samobójstwo przywódca powstania Mordechaj Anielewicz.

23. Ostatnim pomnikiem, który znajduje się na „Trakcie Pamięci, Męczeństwa i Walki Żydów" jest „Umschlagplatz", miejsce selekcji i wywozu Żydów do obozów koncentracyjnych i śmierci. Z getta do obozów, głównie Treblinki, wywieziono około 300.000 Żydów. Pomnik „Umschlagplatz" został umiejscowiony obok budynku, w którym znajdował się czasowy szpital dla Żydów, którzy następnie byli wywożeni do obozów.

WARSAW (GB)

This handful of photographs presents Warsaw at the end of World War II.

1, 2, 3, 4 - all these aerial photographs depict the destroyed centre of Warsaw.

5. Hotel Warszawa located at Napoleon Square, the present Plac Powstańców Warszawy (Warsaw Uprising Insurgents Square). Before the war it was the highest building in Warsaw, occupied by „Prudential" Insurance Company.

6. St. Alexander's Church located at Plac Trzech Krzyży (Three Crosses Square), in the vicinity of which Sheraton Hotel was built in 1996.

7. The Palace of Culture and Science, erected in 1955 as a gift to Warsaw from the USSR, neighbouring with the destroyed Śródmieście Railway Station in the city centre (photograph in the upper right hand corner).

8. Holy Cross Church and the monument of Nicolaus Copernicus. The church is well known in Warsaw and is an interesting tourist site, as the urn with the heart of Frederic Chopin rests there.

9. St. Anne's Church at Krakowskie Przedmieście street. The Old Town with the column of King Sigismund III Vasa appears in the background.

10. The Royal Castle. Its reconstruction started in the nineteen-seventies and is still in progress. In the background: St. Anne's Church and bell tower.

11. The Old Town - Świętojańska Street.

12. The Old Town Market Square - Barss side.

13. The Old Town Market Square - Dekert side.

14. The Garrison Church. It is located opposite to the monument of the Warsaw Uprising at Długa Street.

15. St. Florian's Church, located next to the Warsaw Zoo, on the other side of the Vistula river at Aleja Solidarności (Solidarity Avenue).

16. The site of the Ghetto. St. Augustine's Church which appears on this photograph was in the centre of the Ghetto in the years 1942-1943.

17. The destroyed main streets of the Ghetto: Gęsia Street, Zamenhofa Street, Nalewki Street.

18. The monument to the Heroes of the Ghetto, next to the crossing of Zamenhofa Street and Anielewicza Street. It was erected in 1948 according to design by Marek Suzin. The sculptures in low relief are the work of Natan Rapoport.

19. A general view of the Ghetto area.

20. The first monument to the tragedy of the Warsaw Jews was erected in 1946 on the third anniversary of the outbreak of the Jewish Uprising.

21. A Polish-American committee contributed to the unveiling in 1995 of a granite block commemorating the underground „Żegota" organisation, which provided covert support to the Jews during the Nazi occupation of Poland. The assistance was financed by the Polish Government in exile in London.

The monuments on photographs 20, 21 are located in the vicinity of the monument commemorating the Heroes of the Ghetto.

That site is the starting point of the „Martyrdom Commemoration Route", which consists of 19 commemorating plates and stone blocks referring to significant events and Jewish personalities of the time of the Warsaw Ghetto.

22. The bunker of Mordechaj Anielewicz near the crossing of Dubois Street and Miła Street. A mound with a commemorative stone block marks the location of the bunker which served as headquarters of the staff commanding the Jewish Uprising, known as 18 Miła Street, where Mordechaj Anielewicz, the commander of the Uprising, committed suicide on May 8, 1943.

23. The last monument of the „Martyrdom Commemoration Route" commemorates the „Umschlagplatz", the place where the Jews were selected for deportation to the concentration and death camps. Approximately 300,000 Jews were taken from the Ghetto to the extermination camps, mainly to Treblinka. The „Umschlagplatz" monument is located next to the building which housed a provisional hospital for the Jews, who were subsequently taken to the death camps.

Ⓓ WARSCHAU

Anhand einiger Fotografien möchten wir Warschau nach Kriegsende zeigen.

1,2,3,4 - alle Luftaufnahmen zeigen das zerstörte Zentrum Warschaus.

5. Das Hotel "Warszawa" befand sich auf dem Napoleonsplatz, dem heutigen Platz der Warschauer Aufständischen. Vor dem Krieg das höchste Gebäude Warschaus, in dem die Versicherungsgesellschaft „Prudential" ihren Sitz hatte.
6. Die Alexanderkirche befindet sich auf dem Dreikreuzeplatz , neben dem 1996 das Hotel „Sheraton" errichtet wurde.
7. Der Palast der Kultur und Wissenschaft entstand 1955 als Geschenk der UdSSR f(r Warschau, gleich neben dem zerstörten Bahnhof Warschau-Mitte (Foto rechts oben).
8. Die Kreuzkirche und das Nicolaus-Copernicus-Denkmal, eine bekannte Warschauer Kirche, auch für Touristen interessant, denn darin befindet sich die Urne mit dem Herzen Fryderyk Chopins.
9. Die Annenkirche in der Krakowskie-Przedmieście-Straße. Im Hintergrund die Altstadt mit der Säule des Königs Sigismund III. Vasa.
10. Das Königsschloß, dessen Wiederaufbau in den siebziger Jahren begonnen wurde und bis heute dauert. Im Hintergrund der Glockenturm und die Annenkirche.
11. Die Altstadt - die Świętojańska-Straße mit dem Altmarkt (Barss-Seite).
12. Altmarkt - Barss-Seite.
13. Altstadtmarkt - Dekert-Seite.
14. Die Garnisonskirche befindet sich genau gegenüber dem Denkmal zu Ehren des Warschauer Aufstands in der Długa-Straße.
15. Die Florianskirche steht auf der anderen Weichselseite neben dem Warschauer Zoo in der Solidarności-Allee.
16. Das Ghettogelände - die Augustinkirche, die sich in den Jahren 1942-1943 im Zentrum des Ghettos befand.
17. Das Ghettogelände - die zerstörten Hauptstraßen: die Gęsia-, die Zamenhofa- und die Nalewki-Straße.
18. An der Kreuzung Zamenhofa- und Anieliewicza-Straße wurde 1948 das Denkmal zu Ehren des Helden des Ghettos nach einem Entwurf von Marek Suzin enthüllt. Die Flachreliefs stammen von Nathan Rappoport.
19. Das Ghettogelände - allgemeine Ansicht.
20. Das erste Denkmal, das die Tragödie der Warschauer Juden betraf, entstand 1946 zum 3. Jahrestag des Ausbruchs des Jüdischen Aufstands.
21. Dank dem polnisch-amerikanischen Komitee wurde 1995 ein der Untergrundorganisation „Żegota" gewidmeter Granitblock enthüllt, die den Juden während der Nazibesetzung in Polen half. Die Hilfe war durch die polnische Exilregierung in London finanziert worden.

Die Denkmäler auf den Fotografien 20, 21 befinden sich in der Nähe des Denkmals zu Ehren der Helden des Ghettos.

Von diesem Platz aus beginnt der „Weg des Gedenkens und des Martyriums". Er besteht aus 19 Tafeln und Steinblöcken, die wichtige Ereignisse und die Juden während des Bestehens des Warschauer Ghettos zeigen.

22. Der Bunker Mordechaj Anieliewicz' - an der Kreuzung der Dubois- und der Miła-Straße befindet sich ein Hügel mit einem Gedenkstein. Während des Aufstands befand sich hier der Stabsbunker des Jüdischen Aufstands, die sog. Miła-Str. 18. An dieser Stelle beging der Führer des Aufstands, Mordechaj Anielewicz, am 8. Mai 1943 Selbstmord.
23. Das letzte Denkmal auf dem „Weg des Gedenkens und des Martyriums" ist der „Umschlagplatz", der Ort der Selektion und Deportation der Juden in die Konzentrationslager und in den Tod. Aus dem Ghetto wurden rund 300 000 Juden in die Lager, hauptsächlich nach Treblinka, gebracht., Das Denkmal „Umschlagplatz" wurde neben das Gebäude gestellt, in dem sich das zeitweilige Krankenhaus für die Juden befand, die dann in die Lager deportiert wurden.

WARSCHAU

Met behulp van enige foto's willen wij u Warschau na de Tweede Wereldoorlog voorstellen.

1, 2, 3, 4 - alle luchtfoto's stellen het verwoeste stadtcentrum van Warschau voor.

5. Hotel Warszawa - het gebouw stond op het Napoleonplein, vandaag draagt dit plein de naam van de Opstandigers van Warschau. Voor de oorlog was dit het hoogste gebouw te Warschau, met de zetel van de verzekeringsmaatschappij „Prudential".

6. St.-Alexanderkerk bevindt zich op het plein Plac Trzech Krzyży (Het Drie-Kruis-Plein) waar in 1996 het Hotel Sheraton werd gebouwd.

7. Het Paleis van Cultuur en Wetenschappen - direkt bij het Station „Binnenstad" (foto rechts boven) - ontstond 1955 als geschenk van de Sovjetunie voor Warschau

8. De kerk van het Heilige Kruis en het monument van Nicolaus Copernicus - de kerk is bekend in Warschau; ook interessant voor touristen, omdat zich daar de urn met het hart van Chopin bevindt.

9. St.- Annakerk - in de Krakowskie Przedmieście-straat. In de achtergrond is de Oude Stad met de zuil van koning Sigismond III Vasa zichtbaar.

10. Het Koninklijk Kasteel - met de heropbouw werd er in de jaren 70 begonnen - de werkzaamheden duren nog steeds. In de achtergrond de klokketoren en de St.-Annakerk.

11. De Oude Stad - Świętojańska-straat (St.-Jansstraat) met de zichtbare Oude Markt (de zog. Barss-zijde).

12. De Oude Markt in het oude stadsgedeelte - de Barss-zijde.

13. De Oude Markt in het oude stadsgedeelte - de Dekert-zijde.

14. De Garnisoenkerk bevindt zich precies tegenover het monument van de Warschause Opstand in de Długastraat.

15. St.-Floriaanskerk bevindt zich aan de andere oever van de Vistula bij de Warschause Dierentuin in Aleja Solidarności (Solidarność-lei).

16. Het gebied van de getto - zichtbaar is de St.-Augustinuskerk die in het centrum van het getto in de jaren 1942-43 stond.

17. Het gebied van de getto - met verwoeste hoofdstraten: Gęsia, Zamenhofa, Nalewki.

18. Bij de samemnloop van de straten Zamenhofa i Anielewicza werd 1948 het Gedenk- teken voor de Helden van het Getto volgens ontwerp van Marek Suzin onthuld. De auteur van de reliëfs is Nathan Rappoport.

19. Het gebied van de ghetto - algemene uitzicht.

20. Het eerste monument gewijd aan de tragedie van de warschause joden ontstond 1946, op de 3-de herdenkingsdag van de Opstand.

21. Dankzij het Pools -Amerikaans Committee werd 1995 een granietmonument onthuld, gewijd aan de odergrondse organisatie „Żegota", die tijdens het nazi-bewind in Polen an joden hulp verstrekt heeft. De hulp werd gefinancieërd door de Poolse regering in Londen.

De monumenten op de foto's 20, 21 bevinden zich in de beurt van het Monument van de Verdedigers van het Ghetto.

Van deze plaats gaat „De Route van de Gedenkplaatsen en het Martelaarschap" uit met 19 stenen tafels en blocks die belangrijke gebeurtenissen en de joden in de tijd van het joods Getto uitbeelden.

22. De bunker van Mordechaj Anielewicz - bij het kruispunt van de straten Dubois en Miła bevindt zich een heuvel met een steen als herinnering aan de plaats, waar tijdens het opstand de bunker van het staf van Het Joods Opstand, zgn. Miła 18, stond. Op deze plaats pleegde de aanvoerder van het opstand Mordechaj Anielewicz op 8 mei 1943 zelfmoord.

23. Het laatste monument op „De Route van de Gedenkplaatsen en het Martelaarschap" is de zgn. „Umschlagplatz", de plaats waar joden geselecteerd en naar concentratiekampen of vernietigingskampen werden getransporteerd. Vanuit het getto werden meestal naar Treblinka, maar ook naar andere concentratiekampen rond 300.000 joden gebracht. Het monument „Umschlagplatz" werd bij een gebouw geplaatst, waar een tijdelijk ziekenhuis voor joden ingericht was, die vervolgens naar de concentratiekampen gebracht werden.

(I) VARSAVIA

Queste istantanee Vi danno un'immagine di Varsavia alla fine della II Guerra Mondiale.

1, 2, 3, 4 - foto aeree che presentano il centro della città distrutto.

5. Hôtel Warszawa („Varsavia") era situato in piazza Napoleone, oggi piazza degli Insorti di Varsavia. Prima della guerra era il più alto edificio della città e sede della Compagnia delle Assicurazioni „Prudential".

6. Chiesa di Sant'Alessandro, situata in piazza delle Tre Croci, vicino alla quale, nel 1966 è sorto l'albergo Sheraton.

7. Palazzo di Cultura e di Scienza (foto in alto a destra), dono dell'URSS alla capitale polacca, costruito nel 1955 nelle vicinanze della Stazione Centrale delle FF.SS.

8. Chiesa di Santa Croce e il monumento a Nicolò Copernico. Il tempio che è di grande valore affettivo per i varsaviesi poiché vi è murata l'urna con il cuore di Federico Chopin, è anche di notevole interesse turistico.

9. Chiesa di Sant'Anna si trova in via Krakowskie Przedmieście (Sobborgo di Cracovia). In fondo alla strada si scorge il quartiere storico con la colonna del re Sigismondo III dei Vasa.

10. Castello Reale risorto dalle ceneri con la ricostruzione iniziata negli anni '70 e oggi tuttora in corso. In fondo: il campanile della Sant'Anna.

11. Il quartiere storico: via Świętojańska (San Giovanni) e lo scorcio della piazza del Mercato - facciata Barss.

12. Piazza del Mercato - facciata Barss.

13. Piazza del Mercato - facciata Dekert.

14. Chiesa della guarnigione di Varsavia situata di fronte al monumento agli insorti di Varsavia in via Długa.

15. Chiesa di San Floriano è situata dall'altra parte della Vistola, accanto allo ZOO, in viale Solidarność.

16. L'area del Ghetto - E' visibile la chiesa di Sant'Agostino che si trovava al centro della zona del Ghetto negli anni 1942-1943.

17. L'area del Ghetto - le vie principali: Gęsia (delle Oche), Zamenhof, Nalewki, in rovina.

18. All'incrocio fra le vie Zamenhof e Anielewicza si erge, dal 1948, il monumento agli Eroi del Ghetto, ideato da Marek Suzin. I bassorilievi sono di Nathan Rappoport.

19. Panoramica del Ghetto.

20. Il primo monumento che commemorava la tragedia degli Ebrei di Varsavia sorse nel 1946, nel terzo anniversario dell'insurrezione nel Ghetto.

21. Per l'iniziativa del comitato Polonia-USA venne collocato nel 1955 un masso granitico in memoria dell'organizzazione clandestina „Żegota" che durante l'occupazione nazista soccorreva gli Ebrei. Gli aiuti erano finanziati dal governo polacco in esilio a Londra.

Le foto 20 e 21 presentano monumenti situati negli immediati dintorni del monumento agli Eroi del Ghetto, dal quale parte „L'itinerario della Rimembranza e del Martirio", lungo il quale sono disposti 19 tra lapidi e massi che evocano eventi e persone degli anni del Ghetto di Varsavia.

22. Bunker di Mordechaj Anielewicz: all'angolo delle vie Dubois e Miła si trova un tumulo con una lapide commemorativa nel luogo dove era situato il quartiere maggiore dell'insurrezione, nel sotterraneo dello stabile di Miła 18. Vi si diede la morte, l'8 maggio 1943, il comandante degli insorti Mordechaj Anielewicz.

23. Chiude „L'itinerario della Rimembranza e del Martirio" „l'Umschlagplatz", luogo dove gli Ebrei del Ghetto venivano ammassati per la tradotta ai campi della morte. Circa 300.000 Ebrei passarono per questo scalo di carico ferroviario per essere avviati allo sterminio, soprattutto nel campo di Treblinka. Il monumento è situato nei pressi del così detto „ospedale" dove venivano scaglionate le tradotte dei morituri.

VARSOVIE (F)

Les photos qui suivent donnent une image de Varsovie à la fin de la Deuxième Guerre mondiale.

1, 2, 3, 4 - photos aériennes représentant les destructions du centre-ville de Varsovie.

5 - L'Hôtel Warszawa («Varsovie») était situé sur la Place Napoléon aujourd'hui dénommée Place des Insurectionnels de Varsovie (Plac Powstańców Warszawy). Avant la guerre, c'était le bâtiment le plus élevé de Varsovie et le siège de la compagnie d'assurances „Prudential".

6 - Eglise Saint Alexandre située sur la Place Trzech Krzyży (des Trois Croix), où l'on édifia en 1996 l'Hôtel Sheraton.

7 - Le Palais de la Culture et de la Science (Pałac Kultury i Nauki), situé au voisinage immédiat de la gare ferrovière Śródmieście (Centre-ville) - photo à la partie supérieure droite, fut terminé en 1955; c'était un don de l'Union Soviétique à la Ville de Varsovie.

8 - L' Eglise de la Sainte Croix (Świętego Krzyża) et le monument de Nicolas Copernic. Cette dernière église est bien connue des Varsoviens et très fréquentée par les touristes qui viennent se recueillir devant l'urne renfermant le coeur de Frédéric Chopin.

9 - L'Eglise Sainte Anne se trouve dans la rue Krakowskie Przedmieście (Faubourg de Cracovie). Au fond, on aperçoit la Vieille Ville avec la colonne du roi Sigismond III Vasa.

10 - Le Château Royal dont la reconstruction démarra dans les années soixante-dix et où des travaux sont encore poursuivis. Au fond: un clocher et l'Eglise Sainte-Anne.

11 - La Vieille Ville - la rue Świętojańska (Saint-Jean) avec une vue de La Place du Marché de la Vieille Ville - côté Barss.

12 - La Place du Marché de la Vieille Ville - côté Barss.

13 - La Place du Marché de la Vieille Ville - côté Dekert.

14 - L'Eglise de la Garnison qui est en face du Monument de l'Insurrection de Varsovie, rue Długa.

15 - L'Eglise Saint Florian est située sur la rive droite de la Vistule, Allée de Solidarité, près du Zoo de Varsovie.

16 - Le site du Ghetto - on aperçoit l'Eglise Saint Augustin qui occupait le centre du Ghetto dans les années 1942-1943.

17 - Le site du Ghetto - rues principales en ruines: Gęsia (rue des Oies), Zamenhof, Nalewki.

18 - C'est à la croisée des rues Zamenhof et Anielewicz que fut inauguré en 1948 le Monument des Héros du Ghetto suivant une maquette de Marek Suzin. Les bas-reliefs sont dus à Nathan Rappoport.

19 - Vue générale du Ghetto.

20 - Le premier monument commémorant la tragédie des Juifs de Varsovie fut édifié en 1946 pour le 3e anniversaire du Soulèvement des Juifs du Ghetto de Varsovie.

21 - A l'initiative d'un Comité polonais-américain, on inaugure en 1995 un bloc de granit en commémoration de l'organisation clandestine „Żegota" qui - sous l'occupation nazie - portait assistance aux Juifs. Le financement de cette action était assuré par le Gouvernement polonais de Londres.

Les monuments des photos 20 et 21 sont dans le proche voisinage du Monument des Héros du Ghetto.

C'est de là que part la Voie de la Mémoire et du Martyre comportant 19 tables et blocs de pierre représentant des évènements et des personnalités juives associés au Ghetto de Varsovie.

22 - Le fortin de Mordechaj Anielewicz; au croisement des rues Dubois et Miła, on trouve un tumulus avec une pierre commémorative sur l'emplacement du fortin qui abritait l'état-major de l'Insurrection du Ghetto de Varsovie sur le lieu-dit „Miła 18". C'est ici que le 8 mai 1943, Mordechaj Anielewicz - le commandant de l'insurrection du Ghetto - se donna la mort.

23 - Le dernier monument sur la „Voie de la Mémoire et du Martyr" est l'„Umschlagplatz" - le lieu de sélection et de déportation des Juifs vers les camps de concentration et de la mort. C'est ainsi qu'environ 300 mille Juifs furent déportés sur les camps, dont celui de Treblinka pour la plus grande part. Le monument „Umschlagplatz" (Place de transbordement) est situé près du bâtiment où l'on avait aménagé un hôpital provisoire pour les Juifs qui étaient ensuite transportés vers les camps d'extermination.

Ⓔ VARSOVIA

En estas pocas fotos queremos presentar Varsovia despues de la II guerra mundial.

1, 2, 3, 4 - todas las fotos aereas presentan destruido centro de Varsovia.

5. Hotel „Varsovia" - se encontraba en la Plaza de Napoleón, actualmente la Plaza de los Insurrectos Varsovianos. Antes de la guerra este fue el edificio mas alto en Varsovia; en el tenia su sede la Asociación de Seguros „Prudential".

6. La Iglesia de San Alejandro - estara ubicado en la Plaza de Tres Cruces, al lado del cual en el ano 1996 fue elevado el Hotel Sheraton.

7. El Palacio de la Cyltura y la Ciencia fue construido en el ano 1955 como el don de la URSS para Varsovia (en la vecindad inmediata de la destruida estación de trenes Śródmieście - Centro - la foto de arriba a la derecha).

8. La Iglesia de Santa Cruz y el monumento a Nicolas Kopernik - la Iglesia conocida en Varsovia, tambien interesante para los turistas, ya que en ese se encuentra la urna con el corazón de Federico Chopin.

9. La Iglesia de Santa Ana - esta ubicado en la calle Krakowskie Przedmieście. En el fondo se ve la Ciudad Vieja con la columna del Rey Sigismundo III el Waza.

10. El Castillo Real - cuya reconstrucción fue iniciada en los anos 70 y se esta desarrollando hasta ahora. En el fondo se ve el campanario y la Iglesia de Santa Ana.

11. La Ciudad Vieja - la calle Świętojańska con la visible Plaza Mayor de la Ciudad Vieja - (la parte de Barss).

12. Pa Plaza Mayor de la Ciudad Vieja - la parte de Barss.

13. La Plaza Mayor de la Ciudad Vieja - la parte de Dekert.

14. La Iglesia de la Guarnición - se encuentra exactamente frente al monumento a la Insurrección Varsoviana en la calle Długa.

15. La Iglesia de San Floriano - esta iglesia esta situada en el otro lado del rio Vistula, al lado del Parque Zoologico de Varsovia en la Avenida de la Solidaridad.

16. El terreno del Ghetto - es visible la Iglesia de San Agostino, la cual entre los anos 1942 y 1943 se encontraba en el centro del Ghetto.

17. Tereno del Ghetto - las calles principales destruidas: calle Gęsia, de Zamenhof, Nalewki.

18. En la convergencia de las calles de Zamenhof y Anielewicz, en el ano 1948 fue iniciado el monumento a los Eroes del Ghetto, segun el proyecto de Marek Suzin. Los reliefes ha realizado Nathan Rappoport.

19. El terreno del Ghetto - panorama general.

20. El primer monumento vinculado a la tragedia de los judios varsovianos fue elevado en el ano 1946, en 3 aniversario del estallido de la Insurrección Judia.

21. Gracias al comite polaco-americano fue iniciado en el ano 1955 un bloque de granito dedicado a la organización clandestina „Żegota", la cual durante la ocupación hitleriana en Polonia les ayudaba a los judios. La ayuda fue financiada por el gobierno polaco, residente en Londres.

Los monumentos presentados en las fotos 20, 21 estan situados en pequena distancia del monumento a los Eroes del Ghetto.

22. El fortin de Mordechaj Anielewicz - en el cruze de las calles de Dubois y Miła se encuentra el monticulo con la piedra en conmemoración del lugar, donde durante la insurrección se encontraba el fortin del estado mayor de la Insurrección Judia, la llamada Miła 18. En este lugar el dia 8 de mayo de 1943 se suicidó el lider de la insurrección Mordechaj Anielewicz.

23. El ultimo monumento que se encuentra en la „Trayectoria de Conmemoración y Martirio" es el „Umschlagplatz", el lugar de la selección y el transporte de los judios a los campos de concentración y la muerte. Del ghetto a los campos, principalmente a Treblinka, fueron transportados aproximadamente 300 000 judios. El monumento „Umschlagplatz" fue ubicado al lado del edificio, en el cual se encontraba el hospital temporal para los judios, a los cuales despues se les llevaba a los campos.

ワルシャワ (J)

この幾つかの写真に基づいて戦後のワルシャワをご紹介致します．

1, 2, 3, 4. 総ての上空からの写真には戦争で破壊されたワルシャワの中心が写っている．

5. ワルシャワ蜂起参加者広場（旧ナポレオン広場）にあるワルシャワホテル．戦前はワルシャワで一番高い建物で，プルデンシャル生命保険株式会社の所在地

6. 三十字架広場にある聖アレクサンダー教会．1996年に近所にシェラトンホテルが完成した

7. 戦争で破壊されたシルドミェシチェ駅（右上の写真）の隣に1955年にソ連からワルシャワ市民への贈物として文化科学宮殿が造られた

8. 聖十字架教会とコペルニクス銅像．この有名なワルシャワの教会には石柱の下にショパンの心臓が埋められているため観光の名所でもある

9. クラコフ郊外通りにある聖アン教会．うしろは旧市街とジグムンド三世の石柱

10. 王宮．70年代に始った修復は現在まで続く．うしろは聖アン教会と鐘楼

11. 旧市街．奥にはシフィエントヤニスカ通りと旧市街広場（バルス側）

12. 旧市街広場（バルス側）

13. 旧市街広場（デケルト側）

14. ドウガ通りのワルシャワ蜂起記念碑の向いにある守備隊の教会

15. 聖フロリアン教会．ヴィスワ川の向こうの「連帯」通りにある動物園の隣

16. ユダヤ人居地区（ゲト）．1942-43年のゲトの中心にあった聖アウグスタン教会

17. ゲト地区．破壊されたゲンシャ通り，ザメンホファ通り，ナレヴキ通り

18. ザメンホファ通りとアニエレヴィチャ通りの交差点には1948年にゲト英雄記念碑が建てられた．スジン・マレクの設計で，浅浮き彫りを造ったのはラッポルト・ナタン

19. ゲト地区の風景

20. ユダヤ蜂起の勃発3周年，1946年に出来たワルシャワのユダヤ人の悲劇を記念する最初の碑

21. ナチスドイツのポーランド占領の時，ユダヤ人を助けていた「ジェゴタ」という地下組織の記念碑である御影石の塊．ユダヤ人のために資金援助を与えたのは在ロンドンポーランド亡命政府．記念碑の除幕式はポ・米委員会の努力によって1995年に行われた

20と**21**の写真の記念碑はゲト英雄記念碑の隣に置かれている．ワルシャワゲトの大事な出来事を記念する19の石碑からなる「記憶・受難街道」がここから始る

22. アニエレヴィチ・モルデハイの待避壕．チブア通りとミワ通りの交差する角には「ミワ18番」と呼ばれていたユダヤ蜂起司令部の待避壕の記念になる丘と石がある．ここで1943年5月8日に蜂起の指導者であったアニエレヴィチは自殺した

23. 「記憶・受難街道」の最終点である"Umschlagplatz"．ここでユダヤ人の選別が行われて，ここから約30万人が強制収容所（主にトレムブリンカ強制収容所）へ連行された．"Umschlagplatz"記念碑の隣の建物にゲトのユダヤ人用の病院があった．彼らは強制収容所へ行く直前ここに一時的に入院されていた．

Ⓟ VARSÓVIA

A cidade de Varsovia após o fim da Segunda Guerra Mundial.

1, 2, 3, 4 – A zona central de Varsóvia destruída.

5. Hotel Warszawa – estava situado na Placu Napoleona (Praça de Napoleão), hoje chamada Plac Powstańców Warszawy (Praça dos Insurrectos de Varsóvia). Antes da Guerra era o edifício mais alto da cidade e era a sede da Companhia de Seguros „Prudential".

6. Igreja Św. Aleksandra (São Alexandre) na Plac Trzech Krzyży (Praça das Três Cruzes), perto do local onde o Hotel Sheraton foi construído em 1996.

7. Palácio da Cultura e da Ciência, erigido em 1955 como presente da URSS para a cidade de Varsóvia, ao lado da Estação Ferroviária Central (fotografia do lado direito da página, em cima).

8. Igreja Św. Krzyża (Santa Cruz) e monumento a Nicolau Copérnico. Esta Igreja é muito conhecida em Varsóvia pois nela se encontra a urna com o coração de Frederico Chopin.

9. Igreja Św. Anny (Santa Ana) na Rua Krakowskie Przedmieście. Ao fundo a Cidade Velha com a coluna do rei Segismundo III Vasa.

10. Castelo Real. A sua reconstrução iniciou-se nos anos 70 e prossegue até hoje. Ao fundo, a Igreja de Santa Ana e o seu campanário.

11. Cidade Velha. Rua Świętojańska (São João).

12. Praça de Mercado da Cidade Velha, do lado da rua Barss.

13. Praça de Mercado da Cidade Velha, do lado da rua Dekert.

14. Igreja Garnizonowy (Guarnição), em frente ao monumento da Insurreição de Varsóvia, na Rua Długa.

15. Igreja Św. Floriana (São Floriano), ao lado do Jardim Zoológico de Varsóvia, na Aleja Solidarności na outra margem do rio Vístula.

16. A zona do Gueto e a Igreja Św. Augustuna (Santo Agostinho) que, entre 1942 et 1943, se encontrava no centro do Gueto.

17. A zona do Gueto e as ruas principais destruídas: Gęsia, Zamenhofa, Nalewki.

18. Monumento aos Heróis do Gueto – no cruzamento das ruas Zamenhofa e Anielewicza – projeto de Marek Suzin erigido em 1948. Baixos relevos da autoria de Nathan Rapoport.

19. Vista geral do zona do Gueto.

20. O primeiro monumento à tragédia dos judeus de Varsóvia foi contruído em 1946, no terceiro aniversário da eclosão da Insurreição Judaica.

21. Em 1995, uma comissão polaco-americana contribuiu para a inauguração do bloco de granito dedicado à organização clandestina „Żegota", que apoiava os judeus durante a ocupação nazi da Polónia. Este auxílio era financiado pelo Governo Polaco no exílio em Londres.

Os monumentos nas fotografias 20 e 21 encontram-se perto do monumento aos Heróis do Gueto. Esse local é o ponto do partida da „Via da Memória, Martírio e Luta dos Judeus" que engloba 19 placas e blocos de pedra comemorativos de acontecimentos importantes e personalidades judaicas da época do Gueto de Varsóvia.

22. Bunker de Mordechaj Anielewicz, no cruzamento das ruas Dubois e Miła. Uma elevação com uma pedra no topo comemora o local onde, durante a insurreição, se encontrava o bunker do Estado-Maior da Insurreição do Gueto, conhecido como Miła 18. Nesse local suicidou-se, a 8 de maio de 1943, o comandante dos Insurrectos, Mordechaj Anielewicz.

23. O último monumento à „Via da Memória, Martírio e Luta dos Judeus" é o „Umschlagplatz", local de selecção e embarque dos judeus para os campos de concentração e extermínio. Cerca de 300.000 judeus firam levados do Gueto para os campos de extermínio, principalmente para Treblinka. Este monumento encontra-se ao lado do edifício que funcionava como hospital temporário para os judeus que, depois, eram levados para os campos da morte.

VARSOVA (FIN)

Kuvien välityksellä haluamme esittää Varsovaa II Maailman sodan jälkeen.

1, 2, 3, 4 – kuvat otettu lentokoneista esittävät tuhottua Varsovan keskusta.

5. hotelli „Warszawa", oli sijoitettu Napoleonin aukiolla (Plac Napoleona). Nykyään Varsovan Kansallisnousun Sankarien aukio (Plac Powstańców Warszawy). Ennen sotaa korkein talo Varsovassa, jossa oli Vakuutuslaitos „Prudential".
6. Pyhän Aleksanterin kirkko (Św. Aleksandra) sijoitettu Kolme Ristin aukiolla (Plac Trzech Krzyży). V. 1996 aukiolla rakennettiin hotelli Sheraton.
7. Kulttuuripalatsi – tuhotun keskusrautatien aseman vieressä (kuva ylhäällä, oikealla puolella), rakennettu v. 1955, Neuvostoliiton lahja Varsovalle.
8. Pyhäristin kirkko sekä (Św. Krzyża) Mikołaj Kopernikin patsas. Kirkossa on haudattu Fryderikin Chopinin sydän.
9. Pyhän Annan kirkko (Św. Anny) Krakowskie Przedmieścien kadun varrella. Taustalla on Vanha Kaupunki ja kuninkaan Sigismundin III Vaasan patsas.
10. Kuningaspalatsi, jonka jälleenrakentaminen oli aloitettu v. 1970. Taustalla kirkkotorni sekä Pyhän Annan kirkko.
11. Vanha Kaupunki – Świętojańskakatu (Świętojańska) ja Vanhakaupungin tori – (Barssin osa).
12. Vanhan kaupungintori – (Barssin osa).
13. Vanhan kaupungintori – (Dekertin osa).
14. Puolanarmeijan kirkko – sijoitettu Varsovan v. 1944 Kansallisnousun patsasta vastapäätä.
15. Pyhä Florianin kirkko (Św. Floriana), sijoitettu Vistula – joensillan toisella puolella, Varsovan eläintarhan lähellä.
16. Gheton alue – Pyhä Augustin kirkko (Św. Augustyna) oli Gheton keskuksessa.
17. Gheton alue – tuhottu: Gęsia, Zamenhofa, Nalewki katuja.
18. Vuonna 1948 muistopatsas oli sijoitettu Zamenhofin ja Anielewiczin (Zamenhofa i Anielewicza) katujen kulmassa. Suunnittelija: Marek Suzin. Kohokuva: Nathan Rapoport.
19. Gheton alue – yleinen kuva.
20. Varsovalaisten juutalaisten tragediaa koskeva ensimmäinen muistomerkki oli tehty v. 1946 Juutalaisten Kapinan kolmanneksi juhlavuodeksi.
21. V. 1995 Puolalais-amerikalaisen Komitean aloitteesta paljastettiin graniittimuistomerkin, joka omistettiin puolalaiselle maanalaiselle järjestölle „Żegota". Sodan aikana „Żegota" on antanut juutalaisille tukensa ja apua. Apua on kustantanut Lontoossa oleva Puolan hallitus.

Kuvien 20, 21 patsaat sijaitsevat Gheton Sankareiden lähellä. Tästä paikasta alkaa „Juutalaisten Muisto-Marttyyri-ja Taistelutie". Se koostuu 19 muistokivistä, mitkä esittävät Varsovan Gheton tärkeitä tapahtumia sekä Juutalaisia.

22. Mordechaj Anielewiczin bunkkeri – Dubois ja Miłan kadun kulmassa on muistokumpu sekä kivi, mikä muistuttaa paikka jossa taistelun aikana (Miła 18) oli sijoitettu Juutalaiskansannousun esikunta. Siinä kohdassa v. 1943 toukokuun 8 päivänä Juutalaiskansannousun päällikkö oli tehnyt itsemurhan.
23. Viimeinen patsas, sijoitettu „Juutalaisten Muisto, Marttyyri ja Taistelutiellä" on Umschlagplatz, jossa tapahtui Juutalaisten lajittelu ja lähtö keskitysleiriin. Ghetosta pääasiasssa Treblinkaan oli viety noin 300000 Juutalaista. Patsas „Umschlagplatz" oli sijoitettu talon viereen missä oli ollut väliaikainen Juutalaisten sairaala ja josta sitten vietiin Juutalaisia keskitysleiriin.

photo 1   This handful of photographs presents Warsaw at the end of World War II.

photo 2

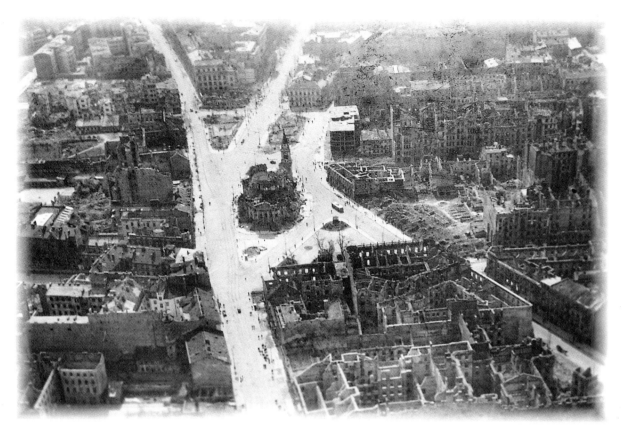

1, 2, 3, 4 - all these aerial photographs depict the destroyed centre of Warsaw.   photo 3

photo 4

1938

photo 5

LIKE A PHOENIX RISING FROM THE ASHES...

Looking at Warsaw today, we cannot imagine the tremendous destruction that occurred in the city during 1939-1944. Nor can we hardly believe that right after the war, the city was just a pile of smoking rubble. Proof of that vast devastation is in the collection of photos of this album, showing parts of the city before the outbreak of World War II in 1945 and after the city's reconstruction.

Warsaw was not the only city in Europe that suffered from the ravages of war. However, its destruction was not so much due to military operations as it was the result of a decision by the Nazi occupants, carried out ruthlessly and methodically.

5. Hotel Warszawa located at Napoleon Square, the present Plac Powstańców Warszawy (Warsaw Uprising Insurgents Square). Before the war it was the highest building in Warsaw, occupied by „Prudential" Insurance Company.

1945

photo 6

It all started in September 1939 with the siege of Warsaw that included bombing from the air and artillery shelling. Some 10% of the city's buildings were damaged and fire consumed parts of the Royal Castle and the Grand Theatre of Opera and Ballet. As if foreseeing the heroic future and dramatic fate of the city, Mayor of Warsaw Stefan Starzyński in his radio broadcast of September 24, 1939 said to the people of the besieged city: "I wanted Warsaw to be a great city. I believed that it would be great (...)

While speaking to you now, I can see it through the window in its greatness and glory, shrouded in smoke, red in flames: glorious, invincible, fighting Warsaw."

6. St. Alexander's Church located at Plac Trzech Krzyży (Three Crosses Square), in the vicinity of which Sheraton Hotel was built in 1996.

7. The Palace of Culture and Science, erected in 1955 as a gift to Warsaw from the USSR, neighbouring with the destroyed Śródmieście Railway Station in the city centre

The *Armia Krajowa* or Home Army was established just before the entrance of the German troops into Warsaw. After a few years of existence, this underground organisation managed to group hundreds of thousands of soldiers. The patriotic resistance movement never stopped operating in Warsaw despite arrests, executions and other repressive measures inflicted upon the Varsovians by the Nazi occupants. Warsaw never ceased to be the capital of Poland, and it was the heart and brains of Underground Poland during the entire period of the Nazi occupation.

According to the Nazi plans, Warsaw a metropolis of one million inhabitants was to become a little provincial town of about a hundred thousand people.

Towards the end of 1940, an area in the central and northern part of the city was delimited where all Jewish inhabitants were to be concentrated. Based on the racist policy of the Nazi administration, that act heralded a future of terror that was to come. Some 350 thoudsand Jews lived in Warsaw prior to World War II, the majority which occupied that part of the city where the ghetto was created.

photo 7

8. Holy Cross Church and the monument of Nicolaus Copernicus. The church is well known in Warsaw and

is an interesting tourist site, as the urn with the heart of Frederic Chopin rests there.

photo 9

photo 9

9. St. Anne's Church at Krakowskie Przedmieście street. The Old Town with the column of King Sigismund III Vasa appears in the background.

Jews who lived in other districts of Warsaw, as well as those who inhabited little towns and villages near the city, were forced to move into the ghetto. Before the 1942 deportation to the death camp of *Treblinka*, more than 400 thousand Jews were confined in the Warsaw ghetto; by 1942, one third of this number had died of starvation and disease.

The ghetto wall, three metre high and sixteen kilometres (ten miles) in total length, separated the Jewish district from the rest of the city.If any of the Jewish residents of the ghetto managed to get outside the walls, he or she could only survive if helped by the Poles. It is estimated that some 20 thousand Warsaw Jews used that help and managed to survive the war in Nazi-occupied Warsaw. Some heroic people like doctor Janusz Korczak (Henryk Goldszmit), a writer and educator, a protector of street children and orphans, would not take advantage of his Polish friend's offer of assistance. He did not leave the ghetto but stayed with his children until the very end: with them, in August of 1942, he boarded the train at *"Umschlagplaz"* (photo 22) and like thousands of other deportees from the Warsaw ghetto, died in the gas chambers of *Treblinka*.

With the whole population of the ghetto deported, the district encompassing

photo 10

10. The Royal Castle. Its reconstruction started in the nineteen-seventies and is still in progress. In the background: St. Anne's Church and bell tower.

photo 10

photo 11

11. The Old Town - Świętojańska Street.

12. The Old Town Market Square - Barss side.

307 hectares (some 750 acres) was levelled to the ground (photos 16, 17, 19.)

On April 19, 1943, before the final annihilation of the Warsaw ghetto, a group of Jewish fighters began a desperate battle against the Nazi troops. This group would rather die fighting than go to death without a protest. On the site of its first clash against the Nazis, a memorial has been placed to honour this courageous group (photo 18.)

Following the siege of Warsaw in September of 1939, the second act of destruction in the capital was the ruthless extermination of the people and the total obliteration of the ghetto area. The third act of destruction began on August 1, 1944 with the outbreak of the Warsaw Uprising. Right after the beginning of the fighting, the Nazis declared that, in retaliation, the city would be totally destroyed. They kept their word: 80 % of the left bank of Warsaw was razed to the ground during the uprising that lasted 63 days; and then, specially assigned Nazi squads burnt and dynamited whatever still remained standing; it was a methodical and well-planned annihilation of the city. Prior to the destruction, the Nazis deported all civilians and imprisoned the insurgents who survived the massacre. Some 200 thousand inhabitants of

13. The Old Town Market Square - Dekert side.

photo 13

14. The Garrison Church. It is located opposite to the monument of the Warsaw Uprising at Długa Street.

photo 14

15. St. Florian's Church, located next to the Warsaw Zoo, on the other side of the Vistula river at Aleja Solidarności (Solidarity Avenue).

photo 16

the left bank of Warsaw perished during the fights and deportations. Meanwhile, the Soviet troops stood on the right bank of the Vistula and watched the city dying.

The central districts and the Old Town experienced the greatest destruction as that was where the fiercest and longest fighting took place. The proportions of the enormous devastation can be seen in the air pictures (photos 1 - 4) taken right after the war. Careful reconstruction of the city is illustrated by the pictures taken during the restoration works (photos 5, 6, 8 and 15).

The Russian troops were approaching from the east. Was it necessary to begin the uprising before the retreat of the Nazi army from the occupied capital? The historians will continue arguing over this subject for years. At that time, the Poles had no doubts about the sense of fighting the occupants and removing them from the capital. They knew that the fate of the city and the whole country was at stake. They also wanted to show their military readiness to regain the country's independence. The Soviet rulers, however, had their own plans as far as the freedom and independence of their immediate neighbours were concerned.

16. The site of the Ghetto. St. Augustine's Church which appears on this photograph was in the centre of the Ghetto in the years 1942-1943.

photo 16

17. The destroyed main streets of the Ghetto: Gęsia Street, Zamenhofa Street, Nalewki Street.

17. The destroyed main streets of the Ghetto: Gęsia Street, Zamenhofa Street, Nalewki Street.

18. The monument to the Heroes of the Ghetto, next to the crossing of Zamenhofa Street and Anielewicza Street. It was erected in 1948 according to design by Marek Suzin. The sculptures in low relief are the work of Natan Rapoport.

That is why they halted the Soviet army offensive and let the Nazis overpower the indomitable city. That is how the third and the last act of the city's wartime tragedies came about.

The Germans left the city in January 1945. When on the 17th of the same month the liberation army entered Warsaw, they found a deserted site with ruins and graves. There was an idea to temporarily move the capital of the country to Łódź, but it was soon abandoned in the face of general optimism and the will to return the capital back to life. Returning people were quickly filling empty streets and ruins. The Varsovians, scattered around the country and deported to camps, were coming back to their ruined homes and trying to organise their life anew. They started with the reconstruction and soon, thanks to their enthusiasm and zeal, the Warsaw tempo of rebuilding became known everywhere, including abroad. "The whole country helps in the reconstruction of its capital" became a nation-wide accepted slogan. The quick healing of the capital's wounds was undoubtedly due to the efforts and sacrifice of the country's other provinces. Therefore, the reconstruction period of the country's capital was basically completed twenty years after the end of the war. There were, however, sites which were reconstructed much later.

18. The monument to the Heroes of the Ghetto, next to the crossing of Zamenhofa Street and Anielewicza Street.

photo 18

For example, the Royal Castle was restored in the early 1980s, rebuilt from scratch to its former splendour. Many historical buildings never reappeared in the city's landscape. Their sites are now occupied by more modern but not necessarily more beautiful buildings.

The monumental Palace of Culture and Science (photo 7), patterned on Moscow's skyscrapers and erected in the early 1950s as a gift from the Soviet Union, is a good example of the controversial Soviet architecture of that period. It was not in harmony with the architecture of Warsaw. In addition, its 230-metre-high spire dominating over the city centre irritated the Varsovians. Towards the end of the 20th century, however, dozens of new glass and metal, super-modern buildings were raised in Warsaw; and the "wedding cake" Palace started to be perceived almost as a historical edifice. People gradually became accustomed to its presence. The Eiffel Tower also irritated the Parisians once...

Warsaw of the late 20th and the early 21th century is certainly not the city that was imagined by Mayor Stefan Starzyński when in the 1930's he and his counsellors designed their vision of a great and modern metropolis. Those plans could not come true because of the war; but ambitions were awakened that enabled the city to survive and to victoriously come back to life.

19. A general view of the Ghetto area.

20. The first monument to the tragedy of the Warsaw Jews was erected in 1946 on the third anniversary of the outbreak of the Jewish Uprising.

photo 20

21. A Polish-American committee contributed to the unveiling in 1995 of a granite block commemorating the underground „Żegota" organisation, which provided covert support to the Jews during the Nazi occupation of Poland. The assistance was financed by the Polish Government in exile in London.

The word "great", when applied to the history of the city of Warsaw, is not only synonymous with "vast" or "magnificent". Warsaw became great thanks to the heroic role it played during World War II, and to the unparalleled endurance that it manifested throughout the reconstruction period. The tragic wartime fate of the city is little known to the younger generation of Varsovians, newcomers from remote destinations or foreigners.

This little album contains a handful of documentary photos which may help you understand the phenomenon of a city doomed to perish; the city which survived its own death and managed to rise like a phoenix from the ashes.

Warsaw's city symbol is the Mermaid; a graceful, half-woman half-fish bearing a sword, she stands ever ready to defend the city; in peace time, her sword becomes a harmless accessory. Were it not the beloved defending Mermaid representing this heroic city, then surely it would be the legendary phoenix bird, surviving its own death and managing to rise from its ashes. The history of Poland's capital reminds us of a Greek tragedy – but with a happy ending!

* * *

22. The bunker of Mordechaj Anielewicz near the crossing of Dubois Street and Miła Street. A mound with a commemorative stone block marks the location of the bunker which served as headquarters of the staff commanding the Jewish Uprising, known as 18 Miła Street, where Mordechaj Anielewicz, the commander of the Uprising, committed suicide on May 8, 1943.

23. The last monument of the „Martyrdom Commemoration Route" commemorates the „Umschlagplatz", the place where the Jews were selected for deportation to the concentration and death camps. Approximately 300,000 Jews were taken from the Ghetto to the extermination camps, mainly to Treblinka. The „Umschlagplatz" monument is located next to the building which housed a provisional hospital for the Jews, who were subsequently taken to the death camps.